SEGMENTS

A Collection of prose and poetry by
members of The University of East Anglia's
Creative Writing Society

Anthology 2019

SEGMENTS / ANTHOLOGY 2019

UEA
Creative Writing Society

The *Segments* Team

Managing Director:	Lucy May
Cover Design & Typesetting:	Olivia Bush
Typesetting:	Chloe Moore
Event Planner:	Ellie Reeves
Social Media Manager:	Eli Court
With Special Thanks To:	Nathan Hamilton Philip Langeskov Adrienne Jolly

Editors

Editor-In-Chief Lucy May

Editorial Board Becca Allen
Roseanne Battle
Abigail Braim
Ciara Bright
Eli Court
Connor Enright
Silas Hand
Isabel Hassan
Electra Nanou
Ryan Norman
Amy Pattison
Max Pleasance
Colin Sheehan
Becky Taylor
Elaine Traykov
Ellie Reeves
Beth Reeves
Ellie Robson

Contents

A NOTE FROM COMMITTEE	*Lucy May*	11
A Moth Hit by a Train	*Angus Brown*	15
Account of a Train Journey	*Silas Hand*	17
Alternative Facts	*Alex Howe*	20
As *n* approaches infinity	*Ellie Reeves*	21
Bells (Stella and Jim)	*Ciara Gaughan*	22
bolognese	*Sebastian Bronson Boddie*	25
Car Park	*Jordan Hunnisett*	26
Chance	*Alex Howe*	29
Clifftop Wind	*Erin Ketteridge*	30
Consequences	*Leia Butler*	33
Driftwood	*Rose Ramsden*	34
Elsewhere,	*Lucy May*	36
Far Away	*Amy Pattison*	39
fck	*Ellie Reeves*	41
Hand on Heart	*Siobhan Horner*	42
I Think You Were A Magician	*Leia Butler*	45
In Sickness and In Health	*Connor Enright*	46
Late	*Gabrielle Copeman*	48
Lucas & Carmen	*Eve Mathews*	49
Suns and Shadows	*Ciara Bright*	52
The Shroom Cycle	*Alex Grenfell*	55
Touch	*Maryam Mohamed*	57
Untitled	*Alex Howe*	58
5 Easy Steps to Ripping Out Your Pores	*Rose Ramsden*	59

A Note From Committee

Sitting in Jurnet's Bar, looking around the cram-packed space, everyone falls silent. The entire bar listens, awestruck, as another writer takes the mic and reads out their work.

Whether it's in Jurnet's, St Andrews Brew House, or a seminar room in the Julian Study Centre, members of UEA's Creative Writing Society always find a means to share their endless talent. This year, we on committee knew that we didn't want such a welcoming and vibrant space to exist only for an evening. We would like to introduce you to *Segments*, the first ever edition of the CWS Anthology.

Even when *Segments* was simply an idea floating around committee meetings, we knew we wanted to celebrate such an endlessly inspiring diversity of writers. We're delighted to have such a gorgeous collection of work to commemorate not only the experience of CWS, but the raw talent that is so regularly seen at open-mics and workshops. As you flick through, expect to meet with poems familiar from oaepn-mic nights, experimental and innovative forms - you might find yourself reminiscing a particular workshop, or stumbling across a hidden gem by someone you didn't even know wrote prose. Even though we call ourselves writers, it took us some time to conjure up a title. When we considered how on earth to properly encompass such a varied array of work, *Segments* was suggested after to the way we arrange our open mics. A sequence of three or four readers takes the stage, followed by a short break, followed by three or four more – each section of an open mic is as unique and unexpected as the last. Just as each of our writers brings their individual work to CWS, we felt that playing with the idea of unique but indivisible parts was very fitting. It had absolutely nothing to do with an intense love for oranges.

Of course, this anthology would not have been possible without the invaluable support of Nathan Hamilton and Philip Langeskov. An immense thanks is due for their direction, advice and initiative, as well as a thanks to the school of Literature, Drama and Creative Writing for the funding consistently provided to our society. We would also like to thank Adrienne Jolly, for introducing us to the fantastic work of Olivia Bush that you find on the front cover. It has also been a privilege to work with our editing board, for whom we have to thank Egg-Box Publishing and their volunteers.

We hope you enjoy reading our anthology just as much as we have enjoyed writing and compiling it. As you turn each page, we want you to think of afternoons spent writing in bookable rooms, evenings spent huddled around a mic, and everybody who comes along, however often. For each and every writer, we are infinitely grateful.

Lucy May and the
Creative Writing Committee of 2019

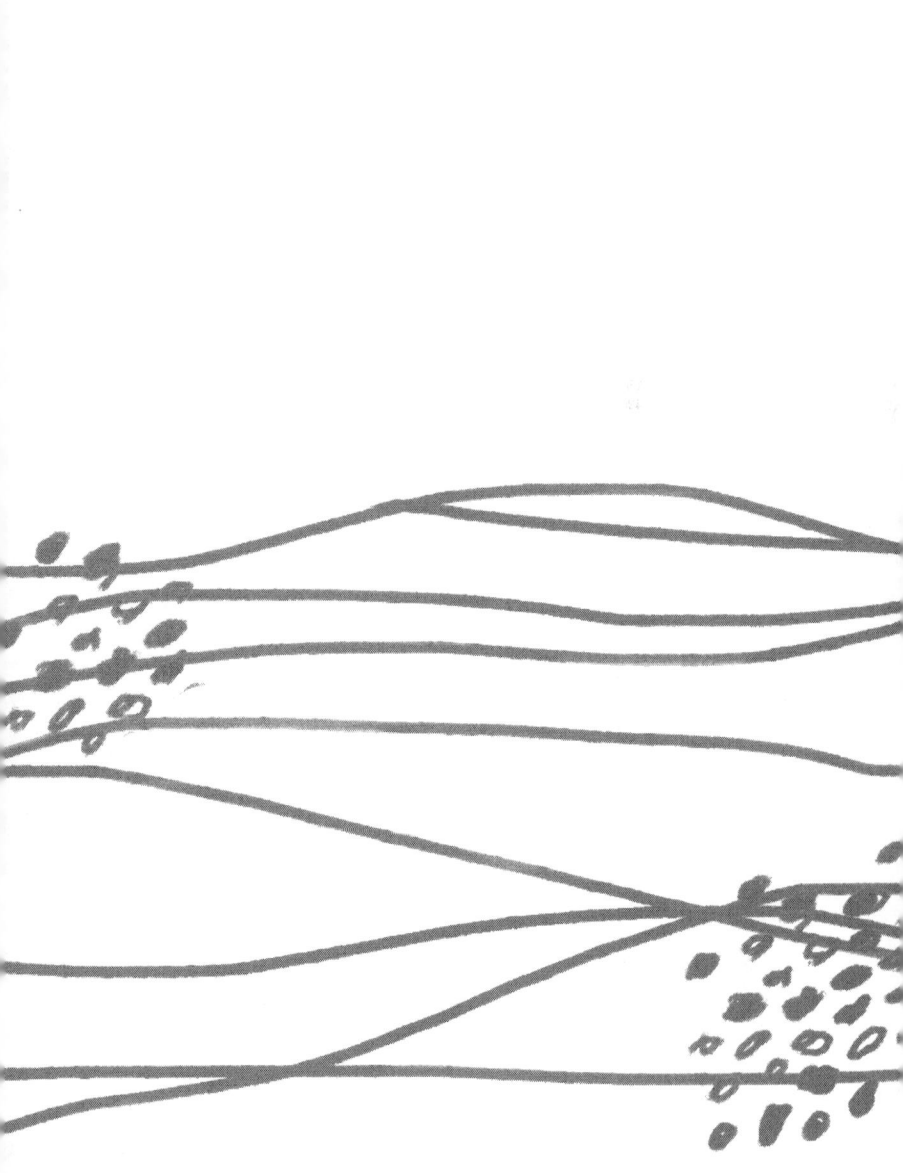

A Moth Hit by a Train
(Additional words by Nick Cave)

Here's
A valley of redbrick; decades' urban decay,
Here's Elysian frenzy; a psychological maze,
Here's banana bread fragrant on long summer days,
Here's Morality shifting in the New Orleans haze.

I move, you move, and one more time with feeling.

See the animals hunching and flexing their brains,
See the masculine card game so bloody inane,
See the primary colours: husband staking his claim,
See boy humble and awkward explaining his name.

I move, you move, and one more time with feeling.

Smell: the sweat of the cautious cloying the gloam,
Smell the stench of the harlot from Sodom to Rome,
Smell the grief on her skin and the gays in her home,
Smell the Samson who's lonely to the marrow in his bone.

I move, you move and one more time with feeling.

Fight the spasms and drinking and pervading slum,
Fight the Stockholm who's happy and he who makes her come,
And smother the past with two glasses of rum,
Fight all that you can and then call you a cunt.

I move, you move and one more time with feeling.

Guess the patience expired and sagacity's gone.
Guess the poems are ended and their promises cons,
Guess this little boy's weak, yes he's overly fond,
When a woman has hurt you, you can do nothing wrong.

A MOTH HIT BY A TRAIN

I move, you move, and one more time with feeling.

Rape the wife who is screaming in hospital bed,
Rape the homeless, the addicts, the once-rich, the dead,
Rape the writer who has written down all that you said,
Rape the one who resists and is messy instead.
Rape the sister: abandoned the day that she wed.

I move, you move and one more time with feeling.

Forget the infant sired of domestic abuse,
Forget cerulean, the Bourgeois, lying faces ceruse,
Forget the best friend sobbing in pathetic effuse,
Forget the damage you've done and your lack of excuse.

I move, you move, and one more time with feeling.

I'm a horse pushing back at the blood-speckled reins,
I'm sprinting through forests and I'm driven insane;
I'm
A concubine weeping it into the rain,
I am the moth who's been hit by a train.

I move,
You move,
And one more time with feeling.

For Tennessee

Angus Brown

Account of a Train Journey

The Boy's feet pound on the pavement, carrying him rapidly, uncontrollably, across an unknown city. Four hours later, the boy is sat on a train, a pen in his hand, considering the best way to express the motion of his feet as they hit the tarmac. He settles on 'pound.' It has an urgency to it; a rhythm. A pounding heart. A pounding beat. A pounding drum? A beating heart? The beat of a drum? Perhaps 'beat' would be better.

The Boy's feet beat on the pavement.

No, 'beat' will not work. The rhyme between 'feet' and 'beat' is too defined, and too rhythmic for his erratic movements. The beat of a drum when you march. The boy had not marched, he had… danced, the beat of the music in his ears carrying him forward.

There it is again – 'beat.' But beat is not right. Can music pound? A pounding bassline. A pounding chest. The pounding of a drum?

The boy silently rolls the word 'pound' through his mouth. It has an explosive quality to it, the 'P' driving it forward, but it is rounded. Pound. Round. The boy thinks about his motion again. The front of his foot hits the ground first. No, the heel does, and it rolls forward onto his toes, before leaving the ground, and transferring the weight to the other foot. The boy wants to know if this remembered motion is correct, but he cannot run down the aisle of the train. Rather, he could; but does not wish to. The more he considers it, the better 'pound' works. His heel is the explosive 'P', hitting into the pavement, and his toes are the rounded 'ound' of the word, an extended, driving pulse, like the bassline of the song which danced through his ears.

The Boy's feet pound on the pavement.

An hour ago, when the train had been quieter, the boy had sat alone, watching the sunset across the carriage. 'Set' describes something hardening, solidifying – but the sun had not done so. The sun's light was slowly pulled apart, the atmosphere refracting it into thousands of colours, the richest of these which passed across the clouds which passed by the boy.

The boy had not watched the yellows surrounding the sun as it passed the western horizon, but the deep reds, indigoes, violets, which had projected themselves onto an eastern bank of clouds. The refracted light had dripped off the clouds like wet paint, and formed a rainbow, a straight line of perfect colour, placed in front of the twisting air. It had not been the complete spectrum of an ordinary rainbow – the refracted light had left it half-complete, but this incompleteness gave an extra beauty to the dripping colour, something unknown and more – profound?

No, the sun had not set, the sun had liquefied, the colours separating like a high-school chromatography experiment, with only the most beautiful, the most fantastic projecting on the clouds and reflecting into the boy's pupils, to be transmitted to his brain, and to be half-described on paper an hour later. At the time, the boy had thought about capturing the colour in a photo, but had thought it would take something away – his memory would exaggerate the beauty, while the stark colours of a photograph would expose the objective reality of a sky that had not dripped, that had merely been the scene of the earth's rotation causing the sun to drop behind the horizon.

Words, on the other hand, words are subjective. Words make different connections across different neurons in different people's brains. It is often said that a picture tells a thousand words, but words can also tell a thousand pictures, a different iteration in the brains of every person whose eyes glance across the paper and discern meaning from black markings.

As the boy creates black marks which create different meaning in different brains, a man not three metres away from him speaks to a friend about 'meaning.' The man speaks with an Italian accent, lacking perfect English grammar, but somehow there is further 'meaning' to what he says, because his language has a different nuance and beat to that of a native speaker. Beat. Drum. Feet. Pound. Heart. The Italian lilt of the man's voice forms the words 'life cannot be meaningless, because if you are looking for meaning, searching for meaning, that is meaning.' The boy smiles. A sense of hope, of opportunity, lies in these words, whether or not they are true to the boy. The boy writes down what the man has just said hurriedly, and reads it back to himself. He finds it interesting how the man repeated, reiterated, rephrased 'looking' into 'searching.' The man's friend quietly responds. His voice is low, quiet, English. As the boy cannot make out what exactly the man's friend is saying, the man's friend's words create less meaning in the mind of the boy than that of the lilt of the man. Whatever the man's friend has just said, the man responds with 'I'm really sure that life has meaning. I'm not sure of many things, but I am sure of this.' The boy looks at the man's face as he forms the words. The face of the man's friend remains unseen, obscured by an occupied seat, as if the man's friend is merely the means by which the boy can come to hear the man's words.

    The boy's thoughts, and the manifestation of these thoughts as little black markings on a page has just been interrupted by a phone call from his friends at a party. Right now, the words of his friends carry less meaning for the boy – they are speaking out of want, not out of need. The man's speech is not urgent, but carries urgency. The boy's words on the paper feel urgent to him. Perhaps they are urgent. Perhaps they are not, and the boy is merely making simple black markings on a sheet of paper to express a pretentious desire for profundity.

    Now five hours ago, the boy's feet pound on the pavement, carrying him rapidly, uncontrollably, across an unknown city.

    The boy is me. But not me. Like the sunset, he is half described, and more beautiful for it.

Silas Hand

Alternative Facts

This is not a poem, I tell you, these are not words,
This is not a poem, trust me, I should know.
This is the funeral of facts, the end of experts,
A eulogy for the era when we listened to each other.
This is the construction of the Other, how same
Becomes different, how Lies and Truth sit next to one another,
Lies buy Truth a drink, they chat, and later,
Alcohol thrumming through the room,
You've forgotten there were ever two.
We didn't know, they'll say, we couldn't have known,
When we pointed out the cracks in our foundations,
That this kamikaze approach would split the earth apart.
Who knew that the new news would reject the noteworthy,
And turn to artificial idols to worship?
This is not how the stories we love are told,
If 'we' is still tangible in the dark,
If we haven't already stepped over the cliff
If we're not already in mid-air, legs flailing, staring at the camera
Before the fall.

Alex Howe

As *n* approaches infinity

A circle captures as it rolls
                Past the moon
And meteors give   way or slide
    Off
A small fish in a small pond smaller now and inescapable
So delicate, consistently enraptures or captures you
Forget which as *n* approaches   Infinity
You lose the four points of
A square could never
Hope for such an innocent touch
Me, I've no sharp edges to prick your finger or cut your wrists
I will – it's in my nature –
Squeeze you first into a small fish
And squeeze still more
Still be still
More   Until your breath joins
my orbit

A triangle has direction   and
A stretched square has a handle   and
You are   not
Two dimensional.   But
You would be a circle.

Ellie Reeves

Bells
(Stella and Jim)

Stella, you're swell. Today is gonna be the day that I get stuck to you, struck by you. By now you should've somehow worked out that you're my glue. I knew when we began anew, that you held my fragmented pieces together in a translucent bond.

Jim's tongue weaved round and around Stella's bright red-lipsticked mouth. Over her imperfect-toned teeth, his own a pearlescent whiteness. He was one of the lucky ones with a dazzlingly smile. 'Some think it's in the genes'.

He kept it in his jeans, for Stells.

Oh Stells, hear the knell of my tolling bell-shaped heart – for it announces our binding's funeral. No, please, listen…can you watch me toil forevermore to please you, wishing once more to be seized in Love? For if not, why did you exile me? Make me your foe? Doe-eyed Stells…Can you hear the bells? My heart is singing, singed by your burning eyes – the periwinkle blue, the cornflower, cowing me into dust. You're my glue – holding the fragments together in a web of your honey blonde hair. You have to stay: I love you.

Stella: 'Jeez, so melodramatic. Save me the melodrama why don't you? Can't be bothered for it today – not up for it today; or any day. Just hush now and go away.'

Oh Stella. Come on home, baby girl - don't hurt me anymore. Be done with me or keep my soul – don't leave me in the liminal state of Limbo. C'mon! Have a heart, I know you do, it pulses blue.

~

The taste of Star Anise. The swells of an ocean. Brooding.

Stella, the bells – ah! The Gods that made you touched, ever so beautifully; made you slightly askew.
Anew the night comes and light becomes dim.

Once Stella's trust was breached, it was very hard to stitch back together the tattered shattered pieces of her. Like a glass heart –

don't leave me hanging.

For this blondie was shaken in the jaws of doubt, and left bereft and limping away. She was mewling, alone and unattended to:

'Enough to scar one for life, wouldn't you say?'

Cheating on her, sleeping around. He said he'd keep it in his jeans, for all his queens:
deceiving them all. But there was only one empress, only one he truly aspired to impress.

So why, therefore, did Jim surprise even himself by being so unfaithful? Stress, commitment-phobia, or the lure of the strobes was too much - the parties, clubs galore, the LURE of them was overwhelming, oppressing….

~

Stella, please darling, you're my glue. I can't live without you.

'I'm sure, am I yet your solvent salvation? Inhale my wintery fumes and get another high, the comedown of which results in affairs? I don't think so…'

But darling Stells, you're my glue – I can't begin anew – I'm transfixed – mix me up inside, I've tried and tried to apologize but each time the ache grows worse, it's my curse Stells, to see the future you can't envision; my pigeon, my cooing dove, my love. Listen, can't you hear the bells? The swells of sound; around my head it grows a tide of sound, a tsunami that submerges me so I feel I'll drown, if you – in your crown – don't seek to reach down off your throne and throw a line to pull me free of the debris of a past slew - of sins. My purging – release me from purgatory.

Steely Stella – I implore you – listen to the bells – swells of tide and the reasons to hide away all of the pain you're feeling – this burning, this bruising: taking over your body entire. Incinerations of the photographs we had – the memories up in flumes of fire, the fumes from burning paper. Through the flames, I see your shame – eyelids heavy and eyebrows fierce.

Ciara Gaughan

bolognese

it's a little untraditional. you ask me to try the sauce, full of real whole tomatoes, minced meat, carrots, and peppers cut thick. maybe a little too wet but it smells good. it fills the kitchen
then bursts into the hallway. everything gold. the table sunset dappled, the plastic kettle boiling,
steam coming off in waves. miniature storm clouds forming under the cabinets, dying and collapsing

into droplets that cling to the wood. we are pressed together at the counter, our edges soft like bread. my shoulder pressed into your arm, my hip mid-your-thigh. there is open
space that we fill with laughter and olive oil and Outkast. the quiet moments ache. nothing
but André 3000 apologizing over and over. i look at you a little closer. your square chin,

your laugh Turkish coffee with fresh cream, your huge earlobes. your boyishness. the gleam
of your bared teeth contagious. the way you held the onion when you cut it,
the curve of your hand around it, your wrist bent at a beautiful angle. the angle at which
you'd cup my face, fingers splayed like spider web. i need to say it, it bubbles up in me; i like

being here with you. in the cramped cold room where we make tea and smile over the rims of our
mugs. our pieces and plates mismatched. you, saying my name like you do, your voice warm and rough around the edges like a home-cooked meal. the sauce just right.

Sebastian Bronson Boddie

Car Park

Coffee.

Thea takes a sip from her flask and, as the smooth, strong substance goes bitter at the back of her tongue, drums her fingers on the steering wheel. Swallowing, she feels warmth in her chest, and then rolls her shoulders, relaxing into the synthetic fabric of the car seat. She sighs, and her breath rises in her face, white and fragile; dragon's smoke. It makes her remember the early days of winter in the yard, where she'd still have to groom the horses even though there was a two-inch blanket of snow smothering the ground. It hasn't snowed for years now. Outside, it's dry and windy.

Peter's hat is too large for her head. Her faded fingerless-gloves, frayed along her thumbs and palms, are too tight. Maybe they were her daughter's, but it's hard to remember. Scratching herself behind the ear, Thea looks through the windshield to the ragged fence about fifty feet away, waiting for the horses to charge by. The flickering, neon-green clock reads 12:58. In two minutes the race will begin. She's watching out for her white one; her mare, Lumi, Thea thinks her name is. That's what she was called when Thea took care of her. Lumi was, and likely still is, a very fast horse – she had a wild side. Thea remembers stroking her hair, plaiting her mane - she'd do it the same as she would her little girl. Thinking back now, she realises that they had very similar hair - soft as gossamer, smooth as water.

She's chosen the best parking spot for watching the steeplechase. There's no one blocking her way. Thea thinks back to before, back to when she used to come here on a regular basis, and remembers the line of watchers along the fence, each of them clutching onto a pair of flashy binoculars, flasks tucked between their thighs. Back then, she used to resent them – never paying, always watching, being cheapskates. Now, not only does she detest them, but sees that – although it may seem like it – she isn't one of them.

If she could Thea would join them on the race course. It's only her memories that keep her out. The memories of *them*. It hurts her heart to ponder on it. But who knows, Lumi might change it all today. Thea's hoping she will.

Just before she takes another sip of coffee, she hears it; the crackled speech of the announcer over the intercom. His voice booms through the speakers beyond the fence, and the hairs across her neck stand on end. She puts down the coffee and lifts her binoculars to her eyes, and focusses.

Thea glares at the crowd in the distance, imagining herself there. Her daughter beside her. Peter holding his beer. A nice glass of red between her shivering fingers. And then her - dazzling, a jewel on the track - Lumi.

The gun fires. The race begins. The jockey's whip their horses and they're off. Thea can't see them, but she knows they're coming and that they'll be there soon – it's a relatively short track, and those horses run fast. Hammering hooves. She can feel a surge in her chest. Thea's pink nails dig into the dashboard. Around the bend they come – she sees them, lightning bolts, cantering towards the bush-fence. This is only the first lap, and she's enraptured already; almost panting in excitement, gnawing at her lipstick, feeling feral, primitive, a cat locked in a carrying-cage. And then, there she is! Thea starts screaming in her car, rocking it from side to side, sending the coffee flying. It spills over the foot-mat.

Lumi jumps – her front legs bend, press, and then lift her into the air. Breathlessly, Thea watches as her hind legs tuck up and her neck shoots forward, making her soar like Pegasus. Her jockey – who knows who he is? – who cares? – he has wide, pale eyes. Thea can tell that he's terrified. He should be. Lumi's *wild*. She lands, her hooves crashing against the earth, and races on, leaving the rest of the horses in her wake. Thea's as dazed as they are.

Blinking, startled, she notices the coffee seeping into the floor. She thinks little of it. Her hands find the door handle; wrap around it; pull on it. The car door opens, bringing a cruel bite of wind, and she steps into the car park. Her heels wobble as she walks down the path. She's so giddy. Something's taken hold of her. Peter's hat flies off because she's moving so quickly towards the main gates where the curmudgeonly official stands in his uniform. He's stroking his whiskers, cradling race cards under his arm. When he sees her, he frowns and steps in her way.

Hurriedly, she reaches into her pocket, her fingers scrambling to find her purse. Thea locates it almost immediately; pulls it from her jeans, almost tearing it open as she ravages it, tugging at every flap and zip. Her old annual ticket sits at the back, hidden underneath the picture of Peter and her daughter – the ones who probably started their day like this, right before he got drunk and took them to the railway. Made himself fall. Made her slip. A zooming train – hit, crushed, bloody. Never to be seen again, or at least, not by Thea. She lost all her courage the day they died. Couldn't even face their funeral. But now she's been liberated, freed from her fear by Lumi, just as she knew she would be. Thank goodness.

Thea offers the ticket to the man, waiting for his approval. He analyses the scrap of paper with fire in his eyes. He takes so long that she starts to fear that he'll send her back to her car, shattering her sudden hopes of retrieving all she's lost.

But he doesn't. Instead he smiles, nods, and steps aside.

She thanks him, weeping, and sprints for the parade.

Jordan Hunnisett

Chance

You can see that she loves her in the way she leans against her shoulder,
Closes her eyes and lets the juddering of the carriage carry her away.
It's in the lightness of her wrist as it clasps the handrail
No muscle tensing or stress in the fingers
Calm painted on her face as steadily as the coral on her lips
Buoyed up by blue eyes and an orange beret
Smile hovering on the edges of flushed cheeks, she could be anywhere.
Tarnished by the lines that gild the sides of her mouth,
The bobbled fabric of well-worn wool,
The chips in red nail varnish, yet
I'd frame them anyway.
In another life, I forget my keys and have to rush back or
I pause a little longer to stroke the cat that sprawls on the pavement
in my path or
I'm late to the station or
I get on at a different carriage.
And I miss it.

Alex Howe

Clifftop Wind

On the third day they decided to explore the Cliff House. They discussed it late that evening, when everyone else had gone to bed. In fits of giggles they had thought about what to do. They decided against the boat and had fitted enough of the puzzles to be frazzled of joints and corners and the inside for now. Yes, they had said. We will explore the Cliff House.

The next morning, after their bowls of cereal and glasses of juice, the three of them wait for Mum, Dad and Jamie to take the Osprey to the bigger boat, and watch from the shore as they bob out to the huge buoy between the islands in the tiny channel. There, they would fish, and anything large enough would be cooked for tea. The rest would be put in the bait barrel, to rot and then lure future fish and lobsters into pots. When the boat was far enough out to sea, the three go back inside for walking boots and raincoats.

They emerge into the sunshine and warm air, to the sound of the sea below them. From their cottage on the island, there is a path through a small field right down to the white sand. Further to the east is their only neighbour, a guy who arrives when he wishes and leaves when he pleases.

The Cliff House sits perched where the sallow grass drops to meet the sea. It has always been empty, and is wonderfully ghoulish. Through the windows where straggly curtains still hung, you can see remnants of bunkbeds and carpets, a stove and wooden chairs. On especially dark nights as children they would tell ghost stories. They would say that the cliff top wind they could hear were the screams of the family that once lived there. They liked to see who could spook the others more – stories of a mad-man and an axe, others about a mother boiling her children alive, each character returning as a ghost.

Today, however, there is less fear. Today there is daylight.

They make the trudge to the house in great comedy. They smilingly act out what they may find – a spirit in a wardrobe, a head in a pot and legs in a baking tray. They laugh and joke and wonder what fish they are catching on the boat. Perhaps Dad will fry it in breadcrumbs and serve it in soft brown rolls again, and they'll eat it with eager fingers.

When they reach the overgrown path that leads them off the Landy track and to the Cliff House's front door, there settles an air of solemnity. Meg, the second eldest, clutches the Vaseline in her pocket. Dominic clenches his jaw so the muscles in his cheek flex, and Alex begins to grind away at the grass with the tip of her boot.

In mute funeral procession they approach. Dominic presses a hand against the wood, knuckle to knuckle, groove to groove. His heart stops as a few last images of cured limbs and glassy eyes flash through him, but the door swings easily, unlatched. The house almost sighs in welcome.

'Thank goodness,' it says, 'I thought you'd never come.'

Strange, thinks Meg, for a house to seem to think like that.

The room they step into must have once been the kitchen. The air does not stir. On the table there are sheets of old newspaper, curled and yellowed, breakfast bowls on the table, pots and cutlery in the sink, dried and rotting food clinging to them. There is dust, inch thick, on every surface. The air seems thicker, slower, intoxicating. Meg shivers, as though the ghosts of whoever lived here before are hurrying past, leaping into the sunlight as they must have done so long ago.

Dominic shuts the door behind them, and warily they examine the furniture. Old pictures and fruit carcasses, remains of shoes and lives abandoned in some awful rush.

In the next room, the living room, the furniture is arranged in odd positions. There are ripped books strewn across the floor and the settees and pictures are slashed, and dust is everywhere again. Through the big blank window at the back of the room, the three can see the bay and the channel that backs onto their house. From the Cliff House, the huge buoy looks smaller, and they can't see the boat.

'I'm very tired.' Alex says. It is more a statement than anything that warrants being replied to, so Meg turns to smile at her understandingly. She feels it too. She is surprised when she finds Alex slumped in a slashed chair instead, feet up on the wretched coffee table, a hand on her face with her eyes closed. The room suddenly feels crawlingly warm.

Meg looks at Dominic, who is frowning.

'I feel it too,' he echoes, 'My legs are heavy. Everything feels heavy since we got in here. Maybe it's all that stuffed up air.' Meg nods as though through mud. That sounds very plausible, and then Dominic sits down too. Meg's eyes want to close and stay closed.

'Who let you in here?' Someone asks. They don't seem too angry. Meg turns her head slowly, slowly, to see a man appearing in the corner, as if leaking from the wallpaper. Dominic and Alex are asleep. Meg is too fatigued to jump.

'Ourselves.' She says, dreamily.

'Can't have done,' The man says. 'Must have been Roy. In any case, you can't stay long – though it might be too late.' He eyes Dominic and Alex sadly. 'The walls here, they do something to you. Yes. Don't stay too long. It will take you far longer to leave. Listen. Don't you hear that?' The man cocks his ear as the room starts to lurch. Meg blinks for a while. When she opens her eyes, the man is melting and crumbling into the carpet. 'That's your father calling you,' he says, 'You've been missing for days.'

Erin Ketteridge

Consequences

Joseph Peters
Met Mrs Fisher
Down by the pier.
Joseph said, 'I don't quite know what I'm doing.'
Mrs Fisher said, 'I just want to get away. You know?'
They went to a cafe nearby.
Joseph bounced between water and diet coke,
Mrs Fisher swirled her spoon into the milky foam of her coffee
was she waited.

Lorna Turner
Met Sally Henderson
At the abortion clinic.
Lorna said,
'I know I'm doing the right thing.'
Sally said,
'One day everything will be different.'
They walked through the double doors,
Leaving lighter.

Joseph Peters
Met Sally Henderson
on the Teacups.
Joseph said,
'I don't quite know what I'm doing.'
Sally said,
'One day everything will be different.'
They spun around and around until the world became a blur of red and white.
Joseph continued to spin as he decided whether he should get off, whilst Sally's heavy shoulders slunk off into the night.

Leia Butler

Driftwood

The mattress sighs beneath our weight
I reach forward, hesitate,
And keep my hands to myself.
Before, there'd be no space,
But the dullness in your eyes
Holds a caution sign
To the barrier of someone I once knew.
Before, I could traverse the folds of your brain without a map,
And glide through your veins like a playground slide,

But that comfort was merely a trap.
We've both thrown too many rocks at each other in
The sandpit to now curl around each other like
Yin and yang.
It should be so easy to hate you
But it's hard when I can trace the trajectory of
The poison you spit to each childhood trauma
Buried away like hastily stashed receipts.

I wish you didn't know each experience that made me want to
Slice skin off my thighs,
And yet, I can't bring myself to regret it,
Because instead of "sorry" and "that's horrible" you reply
"Me too"
And then it's not just me flailing in this quicksand.
Sometimes you drag me into worlds I didn't think possible,
Where smiles and affection are traded like oxygen,
And a bridge is just a bridge.
Sometimes I want to push you off the ledges you pull me off of.
You are both the firewood that fuels the flames
And the bucket of water that extinguishes it.
So when everything is this fucked already,
Is grasping onto this sparkler, exuding so much light and burning me with it,

Going to make much difference?
But no,
I have to let go.
We shouldn't talk.
Even now, I'm already drifting from you,
And that's a good thing I tell myself,
It's good,
Because my hands are black as coal,
As are yours.
Because even if I stay,
Eventually we'll just burn out.
So I guess this is goodbye?
But don't think because I'm leaving
That this is easy.

Rose Ramsden

Elsewhere,

there is a terraced house by the seafront.
It is dusk. It is that stretch of Autumn that collapses reluctantly under November. On a street called Needle, a girl is walking, past the corner shop and the roundabout, towards the high street. Small villages are quiet at this hour. Those with children have collected them from school, they are making tea, they are driving along motorways to get home from work.
Streetlights fizz on.
Her walk takes her East, out towards the seafront.

In the front bedroom of number three Seaview Road, a boy is sitting on his bed. The floor of the room is entirely covered with sheets of paper, arranged so that none of the wood is visible. It fans around his bedside table, across to the desk, all the way up to the radiator, where they crease a little against the skirting board.
In his lap is a notebook. In his hand is some masking tape. Periodically, he leans down from the bed, careful not to nudge the paper, and sticks some of the sheets together, running his thumbnail along the join. He rearranges them. Writes things down, cross-references with a huge, cloth-bound encyclopaedia.
The boy rubs his freckled nose, and checks his phone for the time. At five forty, he begins to carefully fold the papers away, without ripping a single sheet.

What makes a house into a home? Brick and plasterboard hung on a wooden frame becomes a host for memories, the way a skeleton serves a body. A staircase is a spinal column, the corridors arteries. The basement is a beating heart.
On the upturned lip of the front step, the girl knocks on the door of number three.
Shoes on the rack, her socked feet walk through eggshell coloured rooms. Her eyes don't drag as she follows the boy up the stairs. She's already seen the wilting wisteria around the door, she has watched the coat rack in the hallway fill gradually with thicker jackets. From August until now, she

knows how the perpetual melt of the seasons spreads its roots throughout this house.

He leads her to his bedroom. Papers do not scatter when the door opens, they do not lift like inhalation and feather throughout the house. The floorboards are bare. The sheets of paper are stacked and pressed neatly onto the bookcase.

Well? she says.

He closes the bedroom door behind him, and it clicks as it is pressed into the frame. She takes the duvet from his bed, rolls it up, and places it beneath the door like a draught-excluder, like the gentlest of pythons, tucking it into the crevice. Blinds are drawn. The masking tape from earlier comes back out of the drawer, to stick the blinds up against the windows. They ensure there's no space, nowhere that can be seen through. From the street below, the window looks to be dark blue, with an air bubble trapped between the blind and the glass. A blanket hung from the curtain rail means the bedroom now, at quarter-past six British summertime, is in total darkness.

The boy says, *ready?*

And she says, *I think so.*

The room emerges like a photograph, developed slowly in a red room. Peeling out of the dark is a white expanse of desk. A bed empty of sheets. A pale grey cardigan draped over the back of a chair.

On opposite ends of the bed, a boy and a girl sit facing each-other. She is cross legged, he leans to one side, long legs folded beneath himself. The clock on the bedside table shows six twenty-seven, beating digital time.

As gently as you might to brush hair out of a lover's eyes, the girl lifts her hand.

From the creases of her knuckles comes brightness.

She casts the light along, keening to the tips of her fingers and out into the room.

The boy watches.

She summons more. It crosshatches along the backs of her hands, rising from her pores and unfolding along her skin.

She stands up from the bed, and it creeps from beneath her clothes. The light climbs the grooves of her spinal column, her collarbone, her pelvis. It illuminates inside her jaw, her eye sockets, the hinges of her elbows. Her skin begins to heat, her t-shirt gathers moisture; the bedroom is a low-lit cinema, a photographers' den, she is embers in a fireplace.

    From his seat on the pillow, the boy tells her to wait.

    If she looks down, she will see her heart beating through her skin.

Into what is now a gentle gloaming, the boy claps an explosion of colour. Powdering into the air, with snap of his hands comes a steaming a breath of violet. It pales, colours melting like the skin of a fish, drifting across the room towards her.

    The boy smiles. *Try me.*

    She inhales deeply and the colour smells sweet, a sickly coating in the back of her throat. Her arms unfold; shadows leap and dart across the floor, overlapping one-another.

    The evening opens out, cracking like Pangea, to reveal a space unheard of. Their energy wheels like Saint Catherine; it becomes a contest, light refraction overlaid with colour. Sunset orange, cerulean blue. They beam with such lucidity it's as if a whole new morning is awakening in the room.

    Condensation beads up against the windows. The bookcase topples to the floor. A patchwork of shadows and colour make the books crinkle themselves, a meadow bloom across the cotton rug. Out of the wardrobe spills flocking crows. An oblong bedroom has become acres wide, crammed impossibly within the thin terrace squashed between the houses.

The bedroom window of number three faces down into the street. If a passer-by were to glance up, they would only see the disused sparrows' nest, neatly tucked into the awnings. Not a light show. Simply an empty room. The blinds would be up, the curtains open, the bedside lamp switched on.

Lucy May

Far Away

I stand in the middle of a Russian street
There isn't pollution here like there is in London
Breathing doesn't seem like a chore
And it doesn't look like there are any cars nearby
Maybe they've all driven away
I can't remember how I got here
Maybe I took too many sleeping pills on the train
And missed my stop
That seems unlikely
But once I missed my stop and ended up in Liverpool
That was when I was in England
But now I'm in Russia
Trying not to draw attention to the mud in my bag
I'm holding a cigarette
Which is weird because I gave up smoking a year ago
After my lungs began to feel like baskets hanging outside a front door
Except without all the flowers
When I think about that time
About a year ago
I think my whole body felt like one big hanging basket
That once had flowers in it but has since been worn by the weather
Like something that probably should have been thrown out a long time ago
It's raining now
Which is weird because it seems like it should be snowing
Its dripping down the walls
It isn't going down the drains though it's just building up on the pavement
The sun gets further and further away and the whole street turns blue
Nightmares are strange because sometimes they make sense
Once I was being chased down the road by a giant string of tinsel
That was around Christmas time
Once I was falling off the back of the Titanic, but Jack Dawson didn't come and save me

That was during my exams
I'm back in my room now
The sun is where it should be
And it's not even raining
There's not even a breeze outside
The hanging baskets have been thrown out
My mum threw them out
She didn't ignore them
I wonder if that Russian street exists
It probably does
I know it exists somewhere
Maybe not in Russia
But definitely somewhere
I'll go back there tomorrow and see if it's snowing

Amy Pattison

fck

There is a fricative frog in my throat
With a mouth so wide it's gone bug-eyed
I choke choke on its croak.

My concern earns an affectionate stroke
I beckon her closer, move my silence aside
Shush, see, there is a frog in my throat.

She peers down my root, it emits a troat –
Fish tongue tastes sugar and spice, a fresh bride –
I choke choke on its climbing croak.

Soft fingers coax closer its eager bloat
Shivers quiver restless tongue slithers to suck
Hush, rise fish, sensitively flush my throat.

Two fingers jerk down. Fat frog feet block my breath
Brekekekex koax koax[1]
her cruel curl catches my uvula
I choke choke on its croak.

She forces the fricative frog down my throat
If its flushes and gushes are not tight confined
She might croak a choke in her unfished throat.

She might feel a bubble egg bung her tongue
Froggy shivers and quivers too flush to hide
Her plosive yoke swallowed by its croak.

But there is a cricket in her mind
She chirp chirp stutters on its grind.

Ellie Reeves

[1] Aristophanes, Aristophanes' Frogs: A Dual Language Edition, ed. by Evan Hayes and Stephen Nimis, trans. by Ian Johnston, 1 edn (Oxford, Ohio: Faenum Publishing, 2015), p. 35.

Hand On Heart

I'm craning over the banisters, trying to distil into words the rising and falling of the mumblings from downstairs. I pray for an awkward silence, anything to suggest things are not going well.

The sound of guttural laughter fills the hall. It does not belong to my father. This rough guffaw belongs to a visitor from Pakistan who I am to meet tonight, for the first time, in an hour. The smell of sesame seed burfi and halwa drifts up. That's not a good sign. I feel sick.

Retreating back into my room, I snatch the crumpled photo from my bin and study it up close, hoping I might find something there to stop my heart hammering. In the Polaroid a stout man sits, king-like, in a leather armchair. His skin is an old, mottled tree stump. His eyes are milky. His teeth are long. He is to become my husband. Right here, only metres away, the deal is half way to being made. I know it from the chinking sound of Dad's prized Glenfiddich glasses.

I rip the photo into shreds.

'University is not for women,' Dad had proclaimed. 'A good marriage, children – that will keep you safe. I am doing this for your own good. You'll see. Look at your mother and me. We did not love each other when we married, eh? Thirty-five years. What a life your mother has had. She did not go to university.'

He tugged at his paisley-patterned Sherwani, the sign that his mind was made up.

I could not look at him, too afraid I would blurt out the truth, that I was terrified of turning out like Mum: alone with her sit-coms and Rangilo Gujarat FM, waiting for us to come home so she had someone to cook for.

Dad lifted my chin softly with his fingers. I could smell his mouthwash.

'Come my Layla, give him a chance. He has a good business and is from an excellent family. He will allow you some freedoms,

I am sure.' He had taken my hands in his, wrapping my fingers around the Polaroid.

I pulled away, letting the photo fall to the carpet.

'I don't want to be given a life, Dad. I want to make my own,' I thought, looking up into his face. But I could not turn the thought into words. I watched the veins by his temples pulse and his lips draw in tight, his dark eyes inches from mine.

'He's coming Thursday.' The slam of the kitchen door made some leaves fall from the spider plant. Mum flattened out the creases on the photo and handed it back to me, her lip trembling.

The guttural sound of throat-clearing, loud and unapologetic, pulls me back to the present moment. I'm supposed to be changing into something pretty but demure. A dress. Nothing revealing. Doing my eyes. When my mother calls I am supposed to bow my head in respect, speak when I am spoken to and play Reverie, the short Mendelssohn piece I have learnt off by heart. I grab my phone, stare at that email again. Three grade As. 'Bingo!' Mum had said. Proud of me. Clever, not like Sharif. I stare at the As until my vision blurs and the three merge into one. My ears burn with the shame of an arranged marriage to an old man: my friends off to university and me picking out a wedding dress.

I fling open my cupboard and pull out my old suitcase. One wheel is missing from the family trip back to Faisalabad. I seize jeans, tops, my favourite trainers and anything warm. I pull a red sweatshirt on, hook the hood up and catch myself in the mirror. A strange mix of fear and freedom churns inside me. I stop. Make my hand into a fist and curl it under my chin, pose like Rodin's Thinker and stare at myself in the mirror. I tie the hood tight to my face.

When I'm done I click my case shut and have a last look around: star-shaped fairy lights, photos of my Pakistani relatives, my tiny mosaic snuffbox. I shove that in my pocket.

'Bye room,' I whisper. 'I leave the light on, tiptoe down the landing lugging my suitcase to the top of the stairs. I'm already sweating under all the layers. The heating has been put on full so the stranger thinks we're wealthier than we are.

Suddenly the music stops. I freeze, expecting my mother's

soft voice to summon me. Then I hear Bert Bacharach's voice singing 'Do you know the way to San Jose?' Dad's trying to impress. I imagine his face, eager and hopeful.

I can't let him down. I can't see the disappointment in his face. I know the As are my new start. Not a word to Sharif. He'll tell. And Mum? Don't think about Mum. She'll be proud. Her girl at Uni.

The stairwell below is dark except for a solitary strip of light from the TV room – Mum watching old movies, waiting till the men have done their thing. The bitter smell of tobacco hangs in the hallway. Another rise of laughter from the living room makes me jump.

I feel like a criminal.

I stagger downstairs, grab my heavy coat and unlatch the front door, my hands shaking.

Something makes me swing round. Mum stands at the door to the TV room, a dim yellow light forming a glow around her tired body. Her dark kohl-eyes glisten and I think I see the slightest tremor in her shoulders. I almost run back, throw my arms around her. For an instant I wonder whether marrying the stranger will be all that bad.

'Go baby. Quickly,' Mum says, lifting her finger to her lips.

I touch my hand to my heart, like I used to at the school gates. I hurry out the door and disappear down the street with my case trundling noisily behind me.

Siobhan Horner

I Think You Were A Magician?

I believe you must have been a magician,
or how else did you repair her with your charms?
You held her as tightly as the air would allow,
magic radiating out from your sunshine arms.
I'm sure you must have been a magician.
Or how else would you fix a broken soul into a near new condition?

Your words were strange,
leaving your lips in blue swirls and golden shells.
She gazed up at you as you let out more spells in colours of rainbow and pastels.
I'm certain you must have been a magician.
How else could you complete such an impossible mission?

Broken girl with a broken heart.
She laughed at every word you whispered softly in her ear.
Her forest's twisted branches unravelled and suddenly all became clear.
There's no doubt you must have been a magician!
Then again,
perhaps I'm just thinking with too much superstition?

Leia Butler

In Sickness and In Health

Would we see bark left on old oak's trunks
or flesh and freckles under ink
if a lover's gaze could write a name
as they carved initials in

and on, and on, for ever more,
the lovers cry this day,
as each did pace the aisle floor
to give themselves away.

Under God and over bones
of those who said the same,
loved and left for beneath the earth
and then the earth became.

I see standing dead in forests,
I know them as the trees,
think of life, of height and rings,
known more to them than me.

For I know only moments past,
my plans have yet to come
up with trees and down below
the mount, with the setting sun.

So let's set the clocks to quarter to
and watch them wander off.
Think of love, like clouds and sun,
never won and never lost.

And of the moon, its changing face
with distance and with time,
spider webs & bridal lace,
beating hearts & ebbing tide.

Claim to love, where you may love to claim,
take a thought instead.
Think of names you thought to take,
doves uncaged, newlyweds,

if you must choose to take some piece,
find a peace within yourself,
but know what is not yours to keep,
in sickness, and in health.

Connor Enright

Late

A threatening the bus driver kind of gallantry

That he pulled off so easy

The 2:45 to Wisbech his rearing steed

All trembling power and pastel purple plastic

Please keep your feet of the seats

Not personally applicable

Dropping crusted three stripes atop stone grey pleather

For the comfort of other passengers

Squeezed against a soft cheese woman

Upper arm skin sticking

A poorly fitted footie shirt kind of chivalry

Gabrielle Copeman

Lucas & Carmen

Carmen will be here. She never lies, Lucas reminds himself, checking his watch again.

The shadows from the trees dance upon the concrete. Little patches of sunlight appear before the wind moves and they disappear again. He would have chosen a bench in a more open part of the street, but the heat makes any surface unbearable to touch. The street is empty as people have gone to escape the midday sun.

His skin feels drenched. Less than a day in the Bilbao and he has already got through two clean shirts. The small suitcase at his feet is thankfully crammed with clothing.

It's always best to overpack, Lucas could hear his mum telling him, *you'll thank me when you get there.*

And now he is here, having caught the earliest and cheapest flight possible and found no one waiting for him at the airport. He'd tried the number Carmen had given him but had received no answer. After forty minutes of anxious texting, calling, and waiting, Lucas had eventually got a text from her. It was a quick apology for oversleeping along with an address and the suggestion they meet here at noon.

Lucas had looked forward to having a reunion with his sister in the airport, sharing a hug and both of them telling the other how much they'd missed them. Instead, he wandered around the city for a little bit, sometimes taking photos at a couple of tourist spots but mainly sticking to the shade the tall buildings provided.

Lucas scans the street again. There's a large metal panelled building, the walls curved causing the sunlight to bounce off in all different directions. Outside is the giant statue of a dog covered in flowers. Lucas is pretty sure it's an art gallery but isn't sure that justifies the presence of a large flowery dog sat outside the front.

It's living art, Carmen would tell him, as if that somehow made it more art-worthy than anything else.

Can art not live inside? he would have countered.

They would have carried on like this until Lucas

overstepped a line or Carmen got bored and smacked his arm with a tourist's handbook.

Carmen would—*will* be here. She'll be here bickering with him and playfully hitting him with books and relishing in the fact their parents weren't here to tell them off.

He checks his watch again. It's 12:08, which means she could still claim to not be ten minutes late.

The street is quiet. Two tourists walk down the road from the flowery dog statue, attracted by the red Estrella sign that hangs above the doorway of a nearby bar. The sweat on their forehead and silence between them suggests they're about ten words away from breaking into an argument.

They manage to reach the doorway fairly peacefully and one of them leans in, holding the door open for a moment. A faint chatter rolls out onto the street, perhaps they are asking if the place is still open at this time of day. Lucas strains to catch snippets of their questions, could they could grab a bite to eat here too? Where's the bathroom? And, most importantly, do they have aircon?

Happy with the answers, the tourists step inside, the door closes, and sounds of talking disappears with it. A hot breeze prickles Lucas's neck. A stray cat wanders into a side-alley, escaping into the shade.

Lucas rolls back his shoulders, feeling the tension in his muscles loosen. The heavy air hovers around his left ear. He realises what's about to happen too late before someone next to him is screaming, 'FANCY SEEING YOU HERE!'

Fingers reach over to start tickling his chin. As he stands up from the bench, almost falling over his suitcase, Carmen grabs onto his shoulders and clings onto him.

'Let me go!' Lucas shouts through the laughter. He tries to shake her off, but she's had eighteen years of practice to know just how to win a playfight with her brother.

She lets go of him only to immediately pull him into a hug as soon as he has turned around. He tries not to notice how much longer her hair is or how tanned her skin has become.

She pulls back and smiles up at him. He offers back an identical one, big and toothy.

There is a moment of silence, of them just smiling before she pulls of her backpack, dumping it onto the bench.

'Just in case you thought I forgot,' She rifles through the backpack, and pulls out her purse.

'Happy Birthday,' she says, waving it at him.

'You're giving me a credit card?'

'No, you idiot. I'm buying you a drink,' she says heaving her bag back onto her shoulder. 'It's not every day my baby brother turns eighteen.'

'And it's not today either,' he laughs, 'it was a month ago.'

'And I'm sure you partied hard,' she laughs and starts to head towards the same bar the tourists just went into.

Of course, she wouldn't have known that Lucas had an exam the next day and spent most of the night revising. She wasn't there to join in on the takeout their parents ordered, or to join him and his friends when they went to the pub that weekend.

'I can't believe my little brother has grown up so quickly!'

Lucas pulls up the handle on his suitcase and wheels it behind him. 'You saw me at Christmas. How can I have changed that much in sixth months?'

She pauses then.

'Well, you're done with exams, you're off to uni soon,' she says, pausing to glance at his arms, which hang awkwardly by his side. She smirks, 'You've started going to the *gym*.'
She's smiling but her eyes look glossy, like they're filling up with tears. 'I've missed out on a lot.'

Eve Mathews

Suns and Shadows

Harry laces her corset, pulling the ribbon tight and tying it in a neat bow, then plaits her hair, deft fingers weaving the dark strands together more by habit than any concentration. She focuses on the dossier in front of her, instead, blue ink scrawled across the loose sheets spread over the desk. The sketch of an older man with long, greasy hair and a twisted sneer stares out at her from the top of one of the pages, and Harry takes a moment to commit the image to memory before she shifts the pages out of the way, looking for a ribbon to tie her hair.

The suns are setting. Bränna's voice echoes in Harry's mind, the gravel-under-a-millstone tone familiar and comforting, even if it does come with shades of impatience.

I know, Harry says back, tying off the ribbon and snatching her scabbard up from the chair to fix it around her waist. I'm coming now.

In the hall, she makes sure the door to her rooms is locked properly, then heads up instead of down, passing neighbours from the upper floors on the stairs. Mr Summers smiles at her as he hobbles down, and Harry offers a brief nod and tight smile of her own.

I'm almost at the top, she tells Bränna. *Are you ready?*

The only reply is a smug impatience that floods into Harry's head, which she takes as a yes. At the top of the stairs, Harry slips out through the door to the roof and closes it behind her, then skips and starts running: a dead sprint across the roof and straight over the edge of the building.

For a moment, Harry hangs in the air. Then the dirt streets down below come rushing up to meet her and her split riding skirts billow around her ears and her breath is snatched from her mouth and flung up and away from her.

A series of dull thuds, more felt than heard, cut through the twilight, and Bränna sweeps underneath Harry to catch her mid-fall. Harry winces as she lands on Bränna's back, the solid, incandescent red-orange-black scales knocking the breath out of her lungs, and she leans back to stretch her chest out and gulp in as much air as she can.

The dragon's laughter sounds like a rockslide. *Is it really worth the landing every time?*

It's the fastest way, Harry says. *Walking to anywhere with enough space for you to take off would take far too long.*

Gravel crunches in Harry's head as Bränna grumbles, but Harry ignores her. Down below, the city sprawls out like a map, and Harry matches it to the papers on her desk, tracing the route from the tavern on the Western Gate Road to the house on Upper Dearside. There isn't anyone on the path, now, so Bränna circles, high above the heads of the oblivious townsfolk, and the two of them wait.

It's almost morning by the time a crop of greasy black hair stumbles out of the tavern and begins the trek further into the city. He weaves across the street, belching and groaning half-remembered drinking songs. Above him, Bränna wheels around and follows, coasting on thermals with her wings outstretched, keeping quiet, stealthy.

On her back, Harry swings one leg over to ride side-saddle, ready to jump down, and rests one hand on the pommel of her sword, ready to use it.

The man makes it almost to the door of his house. Harry lands dead in front of him, rolling and coming up in a crouch, and he's already reeling back, horror painted across his features. He stares at her, then up into the sky, but Bränna is just another dark shadow in the cloudy sky. For the first time all week, Harry smiles. It feels savage on her face, more like baring her teeth than grinning, and another wave of horror flashes over the man's face.

There's a beat of silence as Harry stands up, unfolding to her full height, scabbard swinging at her side.

'Who…who are you?' His voice is still slurred from the drinking in the tavern, but his eyes are sharp, afraid.

'Was that what Alice Loving asked you when you snatched her from the square?'

'What are you talking about?' The innocent mask he puts on is as transparent as the spring waters in the mountains outside the city. Harry rolls her eyes.

'Or did she just scream, like Josie Peregrine, when you stole her from the commons. What about Bella Jenkins? Or Hannah Collins.'

The man cowers against a lamp post. The oil light flickers as he knocks against the metal. Harry doesn't spare it half a glance, but the shadows in the street jump and the man jumps too.

'How do you know all that?'

'The same way I know their bodies are buried in that lovely garden your wife has been cultivating behind your house.'

'Please don't hurt her! She doesn't know anything! I swear!'

Harry nods. 'I'm not going to hurt your wife.'

The sword scrapes on the scabbard when she draws it, and the man yelps like a kicked puppy. Harry's lip curls. He's murdered girls not even fifteen summers old with no remorse, and only now is he at all concerned.

'Please! Don't hurt me either!' He shakes his head, frantic, looking for anything to save him. 'You have no authority.'

Harry shrugs. 'I'm not with the police, no.' She shows him the flat of her blade, the sigil engraved just below the hilt. 'I'm a knight of the Old Order. We do what the police can't.'

The man's eyes flick up to the sky again and she knows he's heard the legends, the tales of a guild borne by dragons. He's still looking up when she slides the sword between his ribs.

Harry leaves him lying beneath the lamp, staring up at the sky.

The suns are rising.

I know, Harry says. *I'm coming.*

Ciara Bright

Poems from 'The Shroom Cycle'

Cordyceps

In the corner of some half-dusky, soddy cemetery,
A closeted sanctuary, surrounded by
The ghastly moan of the wind,
There lies the body
Of one who lived and sinned,
Sewn into sod,
Of one who lived and loved—

No longer—

But on the hallowed,
Hollow grave, where they put to lie
A hallowed, hollow thing
That had to die

Little flowers, pink and pretty—
Like cordyceps to the ant—
Perch, in full and perfect bloom

Amanita: A Sonnet

I found, in our old yard, when we were together, some mushrooms white
A while back; kept them (all this time!), thought they were right, harmless.
They had a quality unique; their form was beautiful, bright,
They weren't—as you call me now—charmless!
A friend said they were edible; delicious

So, I made them my meal—
Didn't think—like you—they were a chameleon malicious.
But they were Amanita, some poisonous ordeal.

…I realised, as my soul did outpour,
How like this futile fungus you were,
For that same mask of kindness you wore, you tore,
And then revealed yourself, you sick slur.
You are my Amanita, my poison-in-disguise,
Only now, as my body dies, does my mind finally rise.

Alex Grenfell

Touch

It lingers on my skin
like ageing Algae
too thick to remember how it started
too strong to create room for air
and the more she grows
the more beautiful she becomes –
like dancing daffodils with broken petals
that weave through on this earth with
strong necks and dying roots.

It's easy to get through life with a
glistening camouflage that shimmers like
how the sun touches water
But everything in nature dies and is reborn again.
Reborn again.
Dies.

Lives impalpably.

Hands that dissolve in the moisture of the
air, can touch but not feel.
It grows numb with laps of past
memories, tightly squeezed into coves of
rose thorns
used in my defence.

So this vessel I call my body
is always too numb to need touch.
Yet the distant body-prints turn into vines,
slowly twisting around a vacuum heart.

In nature, everything is beauty:
Everything needs to be touched.

Maryam Mohamed

and Brett Kavanaugh is a supreme court judge in America and you do your washing up and Brett Kavanaugh is a supreme court judge in America and you have to redo your eyeliner three times and Brett Kavanaugh is a supreme court judge in America and you redo laundry to try to lose a persistent stain and Brett Kavanaugh is a supreme court judge in America and your dad brings it up as a topic of conversation over dinner and Brett Kavanaugh is a supreme court judge in America and you don't leave the house for a few days and Brett Kavanaugh is a supreme court judge in America and you don't leave your bed for a few days and Brett Kavanaugh is a supreme court judge in America and your tongue has vacated your mouth with no clear date of return and Brett Kavanaugh is a supreme court judge in America and you see yourself silhouetted in Christine Blasey Ford's eyes and Brett Kavanaugh is a supreme court judge in America and you realise how many bars the news have on in the corners and Brett Kavanaugh is a supreme court judge in America and no one else on the bus seems to be mourning and Brett Kavanaugh is a supreme court judge in America and Brett Kavanaugh is a supreme court judge in America and

Alex Howe

5 Easy Steps to Ripping Out Your

Oily skin? Pimples? Black heads?
No fear
With our five step Ultra Clear Cleansing Organic Purifying Power Serum™
Acne scars are a thing of the past!

Spots? Not a problem anymore;
Slather your face in our grapefruit exfoliant,
And we'll get rid of those white heads you abhor!
Scrub away any residue clinging to your skin
And stop those blemishes before they can even begin!

Greasy skin?
Douse a cotton pad in toner
And get to work on those clogged pores clinging to your chin.
Scrape it against the planes of your face until
Oil recoils from your cuticles!

Blackheads?
Smother your skin with charcoal,
Wait for the mask to grasp its hooks into your pores,
And tear out your sebaceous filaments,
Stripping away the layers of your face
Until you're marble smooth and clean!

Pores?
Let the punctures in your face soak in our Pores No More serum
And watch them shrink
In a blink of an eye!

Dry skin? We've got a solution for that!
With our new Skin Revolution moisturiser (On sale! Now reduced to £39.99!)

5 EASY STEPS TO RIPPING OUT YOUR PORES

Your face will be as soft as a petal.
Plus, with my coupon code you can get 15% off!

Now
Don't you feel so much better about yourself?

Rose Ramsden

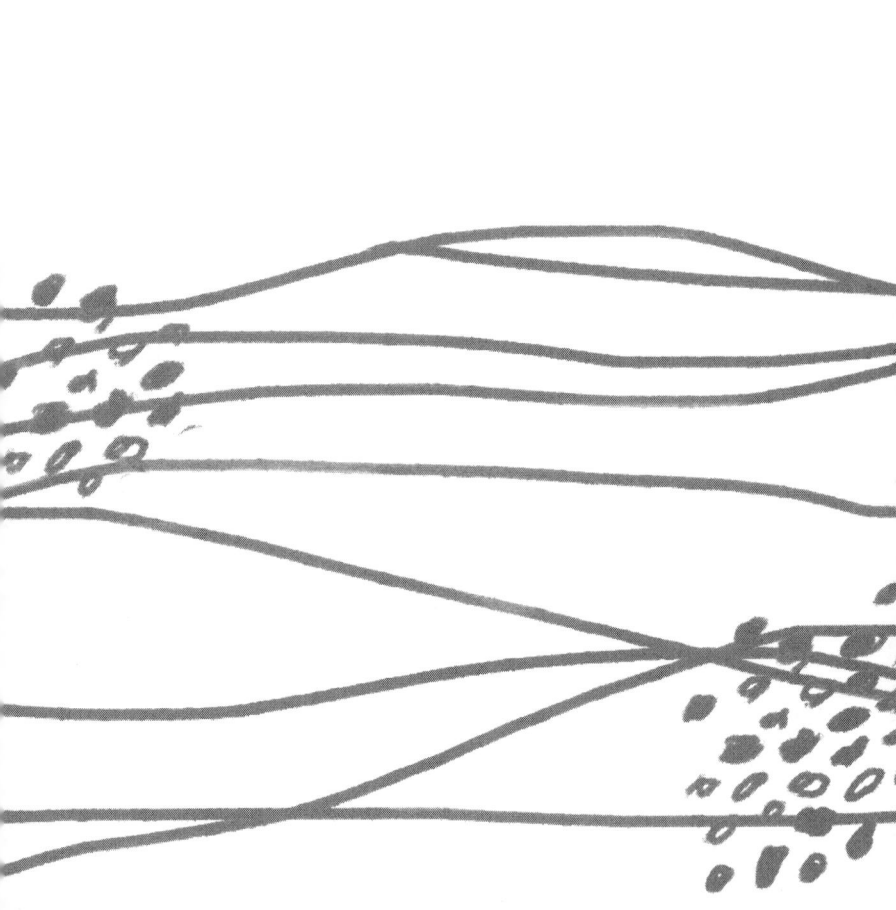

THE UNIVERSITY OF EAST ANGLIA'S CREATIVE WRITING SOCIETY

~

Committee 2018-2019

PRESIDENT:	Lucy May
VICE-PRESIDENT:	Connor Enright
SECRETARY:	Eli Court
TREASURER:	Alex Grenfell
SOCIAL SECRETARY:	Ellie Reeves
HEALTH & SAFETY OFFICER:	Leia Butler
EQUALITY & DIVERSITY OFFICER:	Ciara Bright
UNION COUNCIL REPRESENTATIVE:	Amy Pattison
FIRST YEAR REPRESENTATIVE:	Silas Hand

With special thanks to Nathan Hamilton.
Cover design by Olivia Bush.
Typesetting by Olivia Bush and Chloe Moore.